Ghosts

Ghosts

Stephen Krensky

Lerner Publications Company · Minneapolis

Lerner Publications Company
A division of Lerner Publishing Group, Inc.
241 First Avenue North
Minneapolis, MN 55401 U.S.A.

Website address: www.lernerbooks.com

Library of Congress Cataloging-in-Publication Data

Krensky, Stephen.
    Ghosts / by Stephen Krensky.
      p.   cm. — (Monster chronicles)
    Includes bibliographical references and index.
    ISBN-13: 978-0-8225-6762-2 (lib. bdg. : alk. paper)
    1. Ghosts—Juvenile literature. 2. Ghosts in literature—Juvenile literature.
    3. Ghosts in motion pictures—Juvenile literature. I. Title.
    BF1461.K74 2008
    133.1—dc22   2006101875

Manufactured in the United States of America
1 2 3 4 5 6 - JR - 13 12 11 10 09 08

TABLE OF CONTENTS

Ghosts Step Forward

People have believed in ghosts for a long time. How long? Well, since ghosts are the spirits of people who have died, ghost stories have been around as long as people have been dying. Along the way, ghosts have gathered a lot of

names for themselves—ghouls, phantasms, phantoms, poltergeists, spirits, specters, spooks, and wraiths.

Whatever you call ghosts, stories about them are generally scary. The ghosts appear out of nowhere. They shout "Boo!" at unexpected moments. They rattle chains and moan. Ghosts also give us chills because they are dead. They remind us that life doesn't last forever. When you think about ghosts, you have to think about death.

On the other hand, ghosts can be reassuring. After all, if you believe in a spirit life after death, the idea of ghosts supports this view. Ghosts may not offer the happiest kind of proof of an afterlife, but they show that it is possible. So while ghosts may give us the creeps, they can also be fascinating.

WHY ARE THERE GHOSTS?

Many cultures believe that people have souls or spirits separate from their physical bodies. Even after the body dies, the soul lives on. Some people believe this soul goes to heaven. Some think the soul is reincarnated (born again in a different body). Still others have different beliefs about what happens to the soul. But overall, the soul moving on to the next stage is thought to be a good thing.

Some people believe that ghosts are souls or spirits who can't move on. They remain in their old houses and other places where they spent time during life. But why would a soul remain behind, trying to live its old life? What is holding it back? Perhaps some ghosts have unfinished business among the living. They may want to stay behind to watch over their loved ones. They may want to give warnings about future dangers. Other ghosts may be motivated by anger. They may seek revenge for an injustice, such as their own murder.

A few stubborn souls refuse to accept their fates. Ghosts may become attached to the places where they lived or died. They cling to their former lives, desperately trying to resist death. It's even possible for a ghost to simply not realize it is dead. The soul or spirit wanders through the places it knew in life, frustrated and confused.

HOPPING GHOSTS

Ghost stories are very common in China. People there believe that the spirit world and the physical world balance each other. Some Chinese ghosts are the honored spirits of ancestors. Others are lost souls who need to be guided to the afterlife. But a few ghosts are more troublesome. One of the most famous problem ghosts is the hopping ghost. A hopping ghost is created when part of a person's spirit does not leave the body after death. This spirit, called *po*, is what keeps humans active and vital. So when *po* stays behind in a dead body, the dead body keeps moving. But being a corpse, it's stiff and can't move easily. It gets around by hopping. These hopping ghosts can be pretty gruesome. They are said to have long, sharp fingernails, eyes that won't stay in their sockets, and some serious body odors.

Some people who study supernatural and paranormal phenomenon—events and experiences that don't seem to have a natural explanation—believe that ghosts are energy. In this theory, after the physical body dies, the energy remains and becomes attached to objects or places. Some people think that living people who are sensitive to the paranormal can feel this energy. They sense the ghost's personality or mood, such as playfulness, sadness, or anger.

HAUNTING GROUNDS

Ghosts show up in a lot of places. We've all heard stories of haunted houses—private homes where ghosts roam. Schools, hospitals, and hotels are also common haunting grounds. These are places where many people come and go. The more unhappy people are in life, the more likely they are to end up as ghosts.

Prisons are also said to be haunted. A lot of prisoners have been miserable in prisons, filling the buildings and grounds with negative energy. The most famous haunted prison in the United States is Alcatraz in California. Alcatraz sits on an island in the middle of San Francisco Bay—isolated and windswept. It's no longer a prison. But in its day, it housed more than one thousand hardened criminals. The island and prison have been part of the National Park Service since 1972. Park rangers tell tales of Alcatraz's ghosts. People have heard strange noises at night in the empty prison's cells and hallways. The noises include screams, whispering voices, and the clanking of cell doors. A few ghostly forms have also appeared. Some prisoners, it seems, have never truly been released.

WHAT ARE GHOSTS LIKE?

The prison on Alcatraz Island *(above)* in San Francisco Bay is said to be home to the ghosts of former prisoners.

Ghosts can manifest, or make their presence known, in many ways. Odd noises—tapping, sobbing, footsteps, and music for which there is no logical explanation—are common. Strange smells, such as perfume, smoke, and even horrible stenches, have been reported in haunted spots. In some haunted buildings, the temperatures in a room or in one particular spot will drop several degrees. If all that's not scary enough, ghosts have also been known to move objects. People have reported furniture moving across rooms, paintings coming off walls as if they had been pulled, and even dishes appearing to be purposely smashed. Invisible ghosts who make a lot of noise and move things around are often called poltergeists.

In 1936 two magazine photographers unintentionally captured a ghostly image *(center)* at Raynham Hall in England. Whether it was real, fake, or accidental, the photo's ghost gained world fame as the Brown Lady.

Another common type of ghost is the apparition. Apparitions are quieter than poltergeists. But they're just as scary because we can actually see them. Apparitions can appear as balls of light, swirls of mist, or dark shadows. Some manifest in human or even animal form. When apparitions appear in human form, they look like they did when they were alive. But they are shadowy or transparent (see-through). Often their skin and clothes look gray.

Your Spirit Guide

Here are some brief definitions for common ghostly terms.

apparition: a visible ghost. Apparitions usually take human or animal form. They can also appear as balls of light, swirls of mist, or dark shadows.

ghost: the soul, spirit, or energy of a dead person that remains part of the physical world

ghoul: an evil creature that feeds on dead bodies

haunted: a building, area, or object inhabited by a ghost or ghosts

paranormal: beyond normal experience; events or experiences that can't be explained by what we know about the physical world

phantasm: another word for a visible ghost

phantom: another word for a visible ghost

poltergeist: a ghost that shows itself most commonly by making noise or moving objects. Poltergeists are known to be playful, but not always. Some can be cranky or even downright violent.

specter: another word for a visible ghost

supernatural: events or experiences that seem at odds with the laws of nature

wraith: a ghost that appears in order to warn a living person of a near-future event

Other ghosts are said to look as if they have spent a few years in the grave. They show up as rotting corpses. When people meet a violent end, their ghosts are said to appear as they looked when they died. For example, if someone was murdered by an ax to the head, the ghost will also appear with an ax sticking out of its skull. More peaceful deaths lead to better-looking ghosts. Some ghost stories describe apparitions as beautiful women or handsome men in elegant, old-fashioned clothes.

In some ghost stories, apparitions interact with living people (whether the living people want to or not). In these cases, the apparitions seem to be aware of what's going on around them. They can see living people. In many cases, they seem to want to communicate. Unhappy apparitions have even been said to push or pinch people.

There are also reports of apparitions that seem completely unaware of people. They repeat the same actions over and over, as if they're acting out some event or habit from their past lives. Paranormal researchers call these ghosts residual hauntings. Residual hauntings are common in places such as battlefields. Ghost soldiers there act out the same battles again and again.

Dealing with Ghosts

Many ghosts don't seem to obey the rules of the physical world. They walk through walls and appear and disappear whenever they like. But ghosts are not all-powerful. According to some folklore, people can wear stones such as obsidian to keep ghosts away. Other things can stop ghosts in their tracks too. An iron bar or cross placed over a grave will keep a ghost from rising from its coffin. Salt thrown across the threshold of a door will keep ghosts out of the house. And it is widely believed that ghosts cannot cross running water.

Ghosts can also be outwitted. Some folk tales explain that during funeral services, the furniture back in the dead person's house should be rearranged. That way, if by some chance the deceased's ghost returns home, it will be confused and move on. The funeral procession should also leave the cemetery by a different route than it arrived. That way no ghosts will follow the mourners home.

In English tradition, all doors and windows must be opened after a death to give the spirit of the departed an easy exit. Otherwise, the spirit may remain to haunt the house.

But not all dealings with ghosts are negative. Many cultures have ceremonies and holidays that celebrate the spirits of the dead. The ancient Greeks held an annual festival called Anthesteria. During this time, the departed spirits of a family were invited into the home for a brief meal. After that, the spirits had to leave until the invitation came again the next year. Latin American countries, especially Mexico, celebrate *El Dia de los Muertes* (Day of the Dead) on November 1 and 2. During this festival, people decorate the graves of loved ones with flowers. They leave food and gifts to welcome the spirits.

A man and a young girl *(above)* dress as skeletons for a Day of the Dead celebration in Mexico City, Mexico.

Other countries, including China, Hungary, India, Japan, Nigeria, and Vietnam, hold festivals for the dead. The festival of the dead in the United States and some European countries is called Halloween. Halloween traces its roots back to the ancient Irish celebration Samhain (SOW-en), a day when the spirits of the dead cross back into the land of the living. These festivals honor the memory of departed family members and friends. But celebrators also hope that if they honor the dead on a regular basis, ghosts will leave them alone the rest of the time.

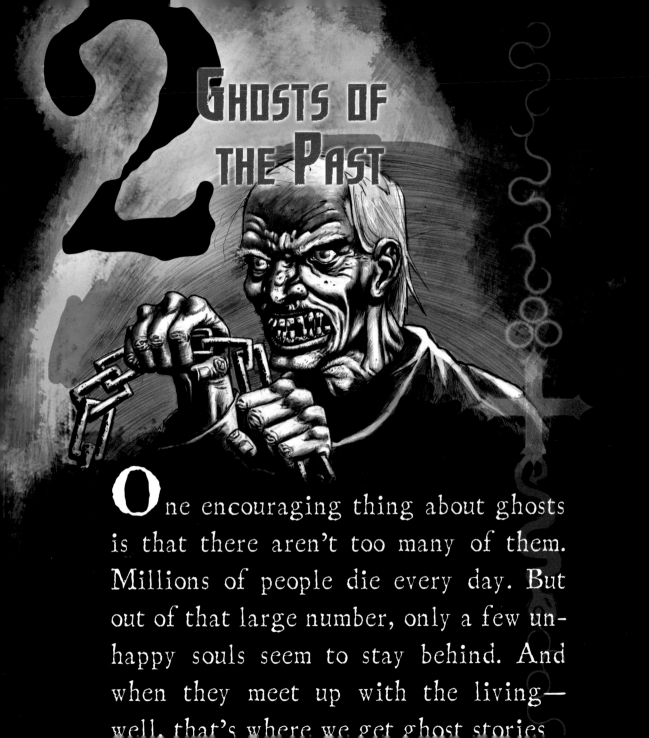

2 GHOSTS OF THE PAST

One encouraging thing about ghosts is that there aren't too many of them. Millions of people die every day. But out of that large number, only a few unhappy souls seem to stay behind. And when they meet up with the living— well, that's where we get ghost stories.

ANCIENT GHOSTS

Ghost stories date far back into history. Ancient Chinese philosophers discussed the nature of ghosts and how humans should deal with them. Ancient Egyptians wrote in detail about the afterlife in *The Book of the Dead.* And in the myths and legends of ancient Greece and Rome, ghosts were common. They appear in great works of ancient literature, such as *The Iliad, The Odyssey,* and *The Aeneid.* These ancient ghost stories have a lot in common with modern tales. The ghosts appear to explain how they died, to demand to be buried properly, to moan that their friends have forgotten them, and to warn the living of danger.

The ancient Greeks believed that the spirit of a dead person crossed the River Styx in a ferry (boat) to get to the afterlife, as shown in this illustration from the 1800s *(below).*

Some of the more popular ancient ghost stories come with a moral. The Roman author Cicero (106–43 B.C.) told the tale of a man named Simonides. While walking along a beach, Simonides came upon the dead body of a stranger. He took the corpse back to town and kindly saw to it that the body was buried in a proper ceremony. Later, Simonides was planning to board a sailing ship when the stranger's ghost appeared to him. The ghost warned him not to board the ship. Simonides listened to the ghost and later learned that the ship had sunk in a storm at sea. The grateful ghost had saved Simonides' life in return for his earlier kindness.

GHOST IN CHAINS

Years later, the Roman writer Pliny the Elder (who lived about A.D. 23 to 79) wrote about a haunted house in Athens, Greece. Each night a ghost appeared and wandered through the house. The ghost was an unhappy old man—thin and pale. He was dressed in rags. He had chains around his ankles, which rattled as he walked. No one recognized the ghostly figure or knew what he wanted. Because of the ghost, the rent was lower than usual. The Athenian philosopher Athenodorus liked the idea of low rent. He moved right in. On Athenodorus's first night there, the ghost appeared. Rather than running in fright, Athenodorus followed the ghost into the garden. There the ghost abruptly disappeared. The philosopher marked the spot and returned to it in the light of day. He asked the local authorities to do some digging on the spot. When they did, they found a skeleton in chains. Athenodorus arranged to have the skeleton properly buried. Once this was done, the ghost never appeared again.

ENGLISH GHOSTS

Over the centuries, ghost stories remained popular, and most countries have plenty of ghostly lore. But one country in particular—England—seems to attract lots of lost souls. Maybe England's big old creaky houses give ghosts good places to roam. Or maybe the country's foggy streets and misty fields provide just the right atmosphere. Whatever the reason, England is home to some of the world's most famous ghost tales.

The White Tower (below) is part of the Tower of London complex. Over its thousand-year history, the Tower of London has inspired many ghost stories.

Perhaps the most popular ghostly location is the Tower of London in England's capital city. The tower stands on the banks of the Thames River in east central London. It started out as a royal fortress in the 1000s and still looks like an imposing castle. But over the centuries, the tower has seen a lot of misery. It was used as a prison for many important people. They included royalty and nobility (people of very high social rank) who had fallen out of favor with the king or queen. Jailers sometimes mistreated and tortured pris-

oners. And some prisoners were beheaded on nearby Tower Hill and Tower Green. With all this suffering, it's no surprise that some of these folks came back to haunt the place.

Tower workers and visitors report seeing some of the same ghosts many times. Ghosts of the 1500s, such as explorer Sir Walter Raleigh, roam the halls. So does the spirit of Lady Jane Grey. This noblewoman was executed at age seventeen, after serving as England's queen for only nine days.

GHOSTLY SCREAMS

Margaret, Countess of Salisbury, went to her death in May 1541. She spent two years as a prisoner in the tower. Her beheading was especially awful. Her executioner was young and inexperienced. He did not kill Margaret with his first swing of the ax. Margaret screamed in pain and terror. She was finally silenced by the ax. But each year on the anniversary of her death, her screams are said to be heard on the tower grounds.

At Marwell Hall in Hampshire, in southern England, an old tale describes the fate of a woman who didn't scream loudly enough. Long ago, on her wedding day, a young bride organized a game of hide-and-seek. She hid herself very well. Time passed, and the game ended. All the other players reassembled. But the bride was nowhere to be found. When her ghost started appearing in the halls, it was clear she was no longer alive. But what had happened to her? Years later a servant opened a large chest in the attic. There she found a skeleton in a wedding dress. Apparently the bride had climbed into the chest to hide and had been unable to open its lid again. Surely she had

screamed many times, but no one heard her cries. Once her remains were properly buried, her ghost was never seen again.

GHOSTS OF THE ENGLISH COUNTRYSIDE

Even England's roads are not safe from hauntings. In Devon, in southwestern England, the ghost of Lady Mary Howard rides in a coach each night to Oakhampton Castle. But this is no ordinary coach. It is made from the bones of her four late husbands. It is said that she murdered all of them. Alongside the coach runs the skeleton of her dog. When they get to the castle, the dog pulls up one and only one blade of grass to bring back to Lady Howard's home. They must do this every night until all the grass is picked, to punish the lady for her evil deeds. But of course, the grass always grows back, so Lady Howard's punishment continues.

In this illustration from the 1800s (below), a family watches in amazement as a ghostly carriage drives past their home.

If you find yourself jumping off the road to avoid a ghostly carriage, hope that you don't jump into the great Windsor Forest in southern England. There you may come across the ghost of Herne the Hunter. As if a regular ghost wasn't scary enough, Herne has antlers growing out of his head. According to legend, Herne was a royal huntsman (someone who organized hunting outings). He served English king Richard II in the 1300s. One day while hunting, King Richard was rushed by a wounded stag (male deer). Herne threw himself in front of the king, taking the blow from the stag's horn.

As Herne lay dying, a wizard appeared. The wizard announced that Herne would live if the king cut off the stag's antlers and tied them to the huntsman's head. Richard did as the wizard instructed, and Herne recovered. The king then honored Herne as one of his favorite huntsmen. But after a few years, the other huntsmen grew jealous and persuaded the king to fire Herne. Herne was so upset over his dismissal that he went out to an oak tree and hanged himself. He has haunted Windsor Forest ever since.

Windsor Forest is part of Windsor Castle, one of England's royal palaces, where the king or queen lives. The castle is said to be haunted by King Henry VIII and his daughter Elizabeth I of the 1500s. Later kings Charles I and George III also haunt the castle.

MODERN GHOSTS

Sightings of ghosts continue into modern times. The reasons these ghosts appear do not seem to change. Love, a desire for revenge, and regret are among the strong emotions that lead ghosts to make their presences known. And ghosts still return, it seems, to right the wrongs they suffered in life.

The White House in Washington, D.C., is said to be haunted by former U.S. presidents Andrew Jackson, William H. Harrison, and Abraham Lincoln.

An Oklahoma ghost story involves a train robbery that took place in the 1890s. During the robbery, one of the outlaws was killed. After the crime, the outlaws gathered at an old house a few miles away to count their loot. They divided the dead outlaw's share among them. Years later, a family moved into the deserted house. They were not aware that it ever sheltered criminals. The family was not there long when they discovered that an invisible presence had started a fire in their stove. Then drops of blood suddenly appeared on the floor. It seems the dead outlaw was still around, looking for his share of the loot. The family didn't wait to find out if the ghost meant them any harm. They packed up at once, left the house, and never came back.

A story from Chicago, Illinois, repeats a familiar theme of a ghost trying to get home. This story begins one winter night in the 1930s. A

This is Resurrection Cemetery, where Chicago's most famous ghost is said to be buried. Local legends claim that the ghost of Resurrection Mary appears at the cemetery gates.

young woman was at a dance with her boyfriend when they got into an argument. The young woman refused to stay with her date. She insisted on walking home alone in the dark. Somewhere along Archer Avenue, a car struck the young woman, killing her. Grief-stricken, her parents buried her in a white dress in Resurrection Cemetery, just outside the city. After her burial, a ghost in a white dress began appearing on Archer Avenue, always trying to get home safely. Chicagoans named the ghost Resurrection Mary. Her tale grew into a local legend, with many more details added. Mary became the city's most famous lost soul.

A ghost also tries to reach his family in a tale from New Jersey. In this story, a woman is startled to find her grown son standing in her bedroom. Her son is a steamboat captain on the Mississippi River, a thousand miles away. He had never mentioned coming home to visit. The two have only a moment to stare at each other before the son vanishes. The woman later learned that her son had died in a riverboat accident at the exact time he had appeared to her. Separated from his mother at the moment of death, the son came home one last time to say good-bye.

3 Making Contact

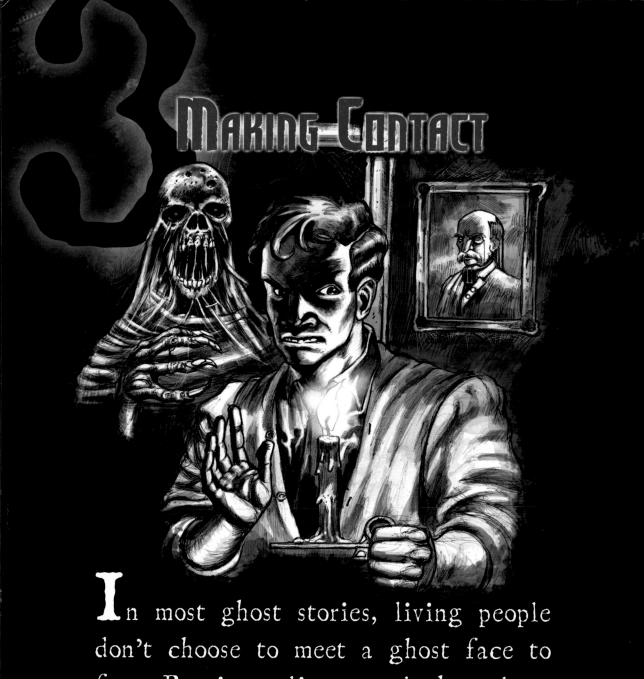

I n most ghost stories, living people don't choose to meet a ghost face to face. But in reality, people have long been interested in contacting ghosts.

Some believe that contacting ghosts allows us to talk to loved ones who have passed over "to the other side." Others believe that ghosts, while unusual, are perfectly natural. These people want to investigate the possible science behind ghostly encounters. Still others don't believe ghosts are real. They try to find logical explanations for ghost sightings. All this interest has made ghost hunting a popular pursuit.

MEDIUMS

Mediums are people who try to bridge the divide between the spirit world and the earthly world. Mediums are said to have strong paranormal powers. They can sense the presence of spirits and understand spirits' attempts to communicate with the living. Those special powers allow mediums to act as "open channels" for spirit messages.

Some mediums make contact with spirits internally. The ghost or spirit simply relays thoughts directly to the medium's mind. The medium then speaks or writes the spirit messages. Another type of medium can trigger reactions in the physical world. When this type of medium attracts a ghost, the ghost will make itself known with knocking sounds, levitations (objects moving or lifting themselves), or the appearance of unexplained lights.

Mediums often operate at séances. Séances are usually organized events at which several people sit around a table with the medium. As everyone concentrates, the medium tries to make contact with a ghost or spirit.

Mediums and séances were very popular in England and the United States during the mid- to late 1800s. Many people at that time believed in Spiritualism. They believed in life after death and that living people can speak with dead ones. Some mediums were true believers who had a real faith in their own powers. However, there were many fake mediums who were in the business just for money. They demanded payment from grief-stricken people desperate to talk to their loved ones.

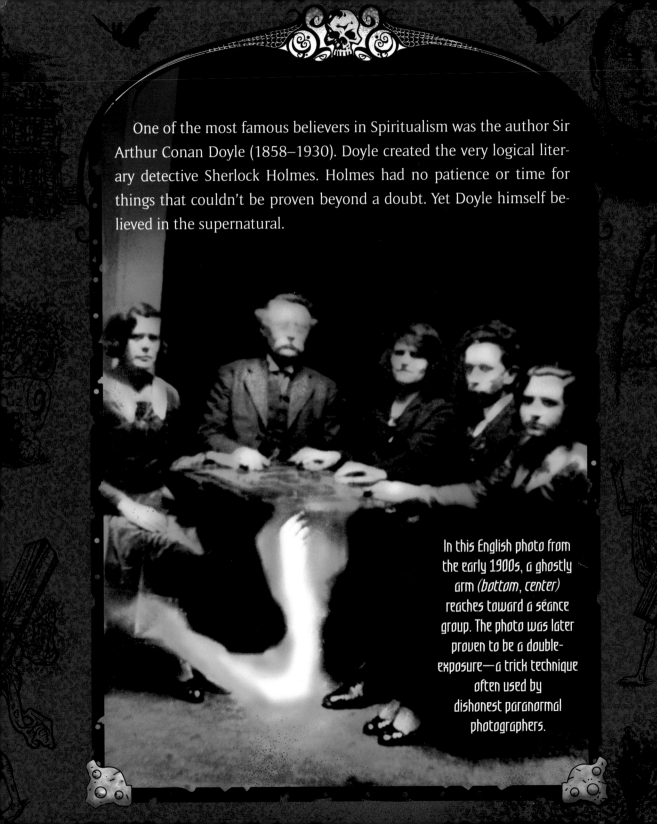

One of the most famous believers in Spiritualism was the author Sir Arthur Conan Doyle (1858–1930). Doyle created the very logical literary detective Sherlock Holmes. Holmes had no patience or time for things that couldn't be proven beyond a doubt. Yet Doyle himself believed in the supernatural.

In this English photo from the early 1900s, a ghostly arm *(bottom, center)* reaches toward a séance group. The photo was later proven to be a double-exposure—a trick technique often used by dishonest paranormal photographers.

THE FOX SISTERS

In 1848 two young sisters, Kate and Margaret Fox, became involved in the Spiritualist movement. The sisters lived with their parents and siblings in northern New York. One day in March, Kate and Margaret told their parents that they had heard rappings in their room at night. The noises were not random. The sisters began interpreting the raps as messages from the spirit world. The Fox sisters became a sensation in the Spiritualist world. They held séances and public demonstrations and made quite a bit of money from both. However, in the 1880s, the sisters confessed to being fakes. They had created the rapping noises themselves, mostly by loudly cracking their toe joints. Later, in another twist,

In this illustration, the Fox sisters *(seated)* levitate a table during a séance in 1850.

Margaret took back her confession. She said she had communicated with the dead. But the sisters' reputations were damaged forever. Spiritualism, on the other hand, kept going strong through the 1920s.

His judgment was probably influenced by the death of his son, Kingsley, in World War I (1914–1918). Doyle believed mediums could help him communicate with Kingsley. He began to investigate incidents of spiritual contact. Others, including many of Doyle's friends, were convinced that these incidents were hoaxes. But Doyle himself never lost his faith.

One of Doyle's doubting friends was the famous stage magician Harry Houdini (1874–1926). Houdini didn't believe in most of Spiritualism's claims. He spent much of his time exposing fake mediums and spiritualists. He did this partly out of a sincere wish to keep these fakes from cheating the public. But he also hoped that someday he might find a real medium who could establish contact with his dead mother. No one ever successfully passed this test, though. If Houdini did meet up with his mother again, it was only after his death.

OTHER GHOSTLY CONNECTIONS

Some people are too impatient to wait for dead people to contact them or for a medium to be a go-between. So they turn to necromancy, or conjuring up the corpse or spirit of the dead by magic. Calling up the dead is no easy task. Past preparations for the event sometimes went on for days. Perhaps the best known story of necromancy is found in the Bible. In the story, King Saul of Israel calls on the witch of Endor to conjure up the spirit of the dead prophet Samuel. Saul wants to ask Samuel about the young leader David, who has raised an army to challenge him. Samuel, however, is not pleased that Saul has disturbed him. And he does not have anything good to tell Saul about his own future.

Not quite as dramatic or complicated is making spiritual contact with a Ouija board. The Ouija board was a game that became popular at the end of the 1800s. The name *Ouija* comes from combining the French word *oui* and the German word *ja,* which both mean "yes." The board supposedly helps users answer questions about the future and helps them communicate with the dead.

The letters of the alphabet, the numbers zero through nine, and the words *yes, no,* and *good-bye* are printed on the Ouija board. The user holds on to a triangular pointer and asks the spirits of the board a question. The pointer then supposedly pulls itself around the board spelling out its answer by pointing to letters, numbers, or words. The Ouija board was especially popular after World War I (1914–1918). Many people tried to communicate with the people killed in that war.

In this 1891 illustration of a biblical tale, the witch of Endor *(center)* calls for the spirit of Samuel, as Saul kneels on the ground.

GHOSTS TAKE OVER

As bad as it might be to run into a ghost, it's even worse to have your body taken over by one. That's what happens in a possession. In ancient times, a possession was considered the work of a god. That means that a god himself or herself actually took over a person's body.

Later, possessions were thought to be signs of evil. Then, according to lore, the Devil engineered the takeover—either directly or through one of his helpers. More recently, though, the ability to possess seems to have opened up to include ordinary ghosts or spirits.

Ghosts or spirits seem to take possession of humans for many reasons. The ghosts usually want to accomplish some task. The ghost might also want to talk through its living host, saying things that the host would have no way of knowing. In some cases, the possessing ghost might even use the person to commit a crime.

Being possessed by a ghost or a spirit is usually no picnic. Often, the only way to get rid of the spirit is to go through a complicated ceremony called an exorcism. In an exorcism, a religious leader, such as a shaman or a priest, commands the spirit to leave. In other cases, spiritual possessions end on their own, as suddenly as they began.

A possessed man (center) struggles as a priest performs an exorcism on him in this 1956 photo. Some people believe that humans, animals, or even objects can be possessed by spirits or demons.

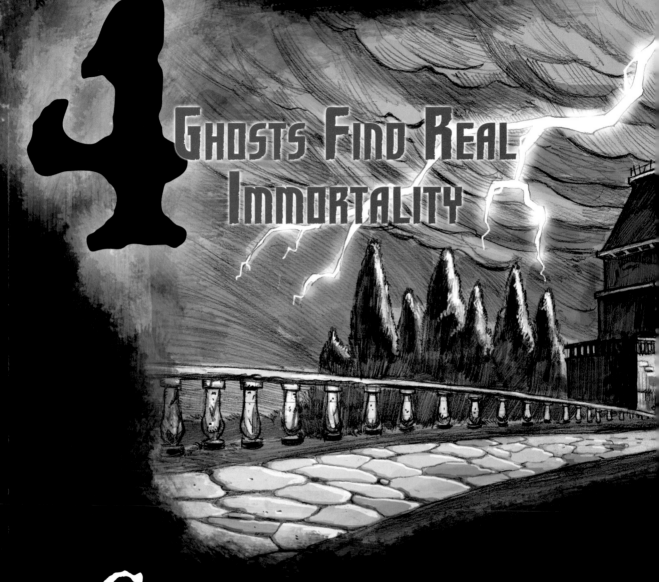

4 Ghosts Find Real Immortality

Ghosts are very popular, so writers have created many stories about them. Some of these stories have lived on with the same immortal qualities as the

ghosts they describe. Few of them are happy tales, though. People, it seems, prefer their ghost stories scary.

GHOSTS TURN THE PAGE

English playwright William Shakespeare (1564–1616) put ghosts at important points in his dramas. *Julius Caesar* (1599) tells the story of the murder of the main character, a Roman emperor. After his death, Caesar's ghost appears to his former best friend, Brutus. But the ghost is not a welcome sight for Brutus. Brutus was, in fact, one of Caesar's murderers.

Murder is also at the center of Shakespeare's *Hamlet* (1601). Early in the play, the ghost of the father of young prince Hamlet appears with a message. Hamlet learns that his father was secretly poisoned by Hamlet's uncle. The ghost's words set the play's action in motion. In *Macbeth* (1603), the main character kills his friend Banquo as part of his plot to become king of Scotland. Macbeth would have preferred to forget about the murder. But Banquo's ghost haunts him with guilt. That's the thing about ghosts. When they think they've been wronged, they can be very stubborn about hanging around.

One of literature's most famous ghosts is Jacob Marley. He was once the business partner of Ebenezer Scrooge, the main character of Charles Dickens's story *A Christmas Carol* (1843). Scrooge is a cranky old man who only cares about making money and keeping it for himself. The ghost of Marley appears at the beginning of the story, as Scrooge prepares to spend Christmas Eve alone in his old house. Marley warns Scrooge that a terrible fate awaits him after death if he does not mend his evil penny-pinching ways. Scrooge is then visited by the Ghosts of Christmas Past, Present, and Yet to Come. They show him how his life was, is, and will be.

In this illustration by John Leach from the original publication of *A Christmas Carol*, Ebenezer Scrooge *(left)* must face the ghost of Jacob Marley *(right)*.

In 1898 American author Henry James published a ghostly novella (short novel) called *The Turn of the Screw.* James lived in England, and that's where he set his story. Its main character is an unnamed governess, a woman hired to watch over and teach a family's children. The governess begins a new job at an isolated mansion. It is the home of two children, Flora and Miles. The other servants in the house hint at some strange goings-on in the mansion. The frightened governess begins to believe that the two children are the targets of a pair of angry ghosts. Are there ghosts, or has the governess let her imagination get the better of her?

Henry James's friend Edith Wharton was a popular and respected novelist. She turned her lifelong interest in (and fear of) ghosts into a collection of short stories. In "Afterward," "The Eyes," and other stories, Wharton repeats many of the themes of ghostly lore. Her stories contain ghosts that silently pace hallways, wake people up in the dead of night, and otherwise give humans the chills.

GHOSTS GET READY FOR THEIR CLOSE-UPS

Ghosts moved easily from books to movies in the early years of the 1900s. For example, *Topper* (1937) tells the story of a stylish, fun-loving couple, George and Marion Kerby (played by Cary Grant and Constance Bennett). The Kerbys are killed in a car accident. But before they go to heaven, they have to perform one good deed. So they return as ghosts to help their friend Cosmo Topper get over his shy and timid ways. *Topper* relied on actors with good physical comedy skills. Roland Young, who played Topper, was very convincing as someone being poked, tickled, pushed, and pulled by unseen ghosts. But the movie also made

In the 1937 movie *Topper*, Marion *(center)* and George *(right)* are friendly ghosts. But Cosmo Topper *(left)* is still less than thrilled to see them.

good use of camera tricks. Long before movies had elaborate special effects, *Topper* featured appearing and disappearing ghosts, see-through ghosts, and floating objects. This supernatural comedy was so popular that it launched two sequels and a television series.

But what about scary ghosts? Well, in *The Shining* (1980), Jack Nicholson plays Jack Torrance, the caretaker of a haunted Colorado hotel. The spirits there are slowly driving him insane. His wife and son end up in danger when Jack goes way over the edge.

If there's a lesson to be learned from *Poltergeist* (1982), it's that building houses on top of an old graveyard is a very big mistake. The ghosts of the people buried there don't take kindly to being disturbed.

When the Freeling family moves in to one of the new houses, strange things begin to happen. The ghosts, it seems, are attracted by the energy of the Freelings' five-year-old daughter, Carol Anne (Heather O'Rourke). At first the family is intrigued by furniture that moves itself and lights that flicker on their own. But things soon go from playful to nasty. The Freelings are forced to call in a team of ghost hunters.

In *Poltergeist* (1982), ghosts contact young Carol Anne *(below)*. Attracted to Carol Anne's energy, the ghosts talk to her through a TV.

Ghostbusters (1984) manages to combine both humor and horror. It is the tale of three scientists (Dan Ackroyd, Harold Ramis, and Bill Murray) and their assistant (Ernie Hudson) who study the paranormal. They find themselves defending New York City against an epidemic of ghostly activity. But an even bigger supernatural disaster looms ahead. What made *Ghostbusters* fresh were the scientific gadgets the team used, such as "containment fields" and "matter streams." The movie introduced the idea of handling troublesome ghosts with science rather than séances.

Beetlejuice (1988), also a comedy, explains how ghosts handle some troublesome humans. When Adam and Barbara (Alec Baldwin and Geena Davis) die suddenly in a car accident, they have a hard time adjusting to

life after death. Then, just as they're getting the hang of being ghosts, an obnoxious family moves in to Adam and Barbara's beloved home. The couple decides to rid themselves of the unwanted newcomers with the help of a supernatural creature named Beetlejuice (Michael Keaton). But with his nonstop talking and bizarre behavior, Beetlejuice becomes as big a problem as the obnoxious humans.

The ghostly appearances in *Field of Dreams* (1989) are much calmer. "If you build it, he will come," whispers a voice to Iowa farmer Ray Kinsella (Kevin Costner). In this case, "it" is a full-sized baseball field that Ray builds in the middle of a cornfield. The ghosts of long-dead former professional baseball players, including Kinsella's father, gather on the field. These are dignified ghosts, with no

The ghosts of long-dead baseball players appear and disappear through an Iowa cornfield in *Field of Dreams* (1989).

desire to frighten. They help Ray reestablish the bond, broken years before, with his father.

In *The Sixth Sense* (1999), nine-year-old Cole Sear (Haley Joel Osment) is haunted by visions of ghosts. "I see dead people," Cole confides to child psychologist Malcolm Crowe (Bruce Willis). Cole's everyday life is filled with ghosts who have unfinished business on earth. He is frightened and doesn't understand what the ghosts want from him. Crowe tries to help Cole. In one of the most famous movie twists of recent years, Crowe discovers he has his own problem with ghosts.

MORE GHOSTLY STARS

Problems are also dogging a young mother in *The Others* (2001). Grace (Nicole Kidman) and her two children live in a large, isolated house on an English island during World War II (1939–1945). Grace's life is difficult. She believes that her husband, a soldier, has been killed in battle. And her

children suffer from a strange condition. They are so sensitive to sunlight that they must stay indoors, away from all windows. Grace hires three mysterious servants to help her, but they all seem to be hiding something. As if all this isn't enough for poor Grace, she soon realizes that the house is haunted. Not until the very end of the movie, however, does she discover who's doing the haunting.

TV GHOSTS

In 2003 cable TV's SciFi Channel introduced a reality series about hauntings. Ghost Hunters focuses not just on ghosts but on the people who look for them. The show's stars, Jason Hawes and Grant Wilson, are plumbers. In their free time, they are ghost hunters. That led them to form the Atlantic Paranormal Society (TAPS). TAPS travels to haunted houses, theaters, restaurants, and hotels across the United States— wherever people have reported ghostly activities. TAPS investigators use high-tech equipment such as infrared video cameras (which can film in the dark), sensitive audio recorders, and tools that measure changes in temperature. The TAPS investigators are true believers in ghosts and the paranormal. But they are not afraid to debunk their paranormal findings—to look for a normal, everyday cause for what seems like ghostly phenomenon.

People who are tuned in to ghostly phenomenon also take center stage on *Medium,* a TV show that began in 2005. Patricia Arquette plays a regular mom named Allison Dubois. Allison happens to hear from ghosts (good and bad) regularly. She uses her ability to communicate with the dead to solve mysteries and crimes. Also in 2005,

In this 2007 episode of *The Ghost Whisperer*, Melinda (Jennifer Love Hewitt, *right*) helps the ghost of a high school cheerleader *(left)*.

Jennifer Love Hewitt began starring in *The Ghost Whisperer*, a TV series in which a woman communicates with ghosts. Hewitt plays Melinda Gordon, who helps ghosts with their unfinished business. In both series, viewers are drawn into the emotional turmoil of the ghosts. But there are always some chills thrown in to raise goosebumps.

Movies and TV shows are proof of our ongoing fascination with ghosts. Maybe some of us just enjoy being scared by a thrilling supernatural tale. Or maybe some of us are intrigued by the idea of an afterlife. Whatever the reason, people clearly can't get enough of a good ghost story—even if it scares them to death.

SELECTED BIBLIOGRAPHY

Finucane, R. C. *Appearances of the Dead: A Cultural History of Ghosts*. Buffalo, NY: Prometheus Books, 1984.

Guiley, Rosemary Ellen. *The Encyclopedia of Ghosts and Spirits*. New York: Facts on File, 1992.

Ogden, Tom. *The Complete Idiot's Guide to Ghosts and Hauntings*. Indianapolis, IN: Alpha Books, 1999.

Phillips, Ellen, ed. *The Enchanted World: Ghosts*. Alexandria, VA: Time-Life Books, 1984.

Reynolds, James. *Gallery of Ghosts*. New York: Grossett and Dunlap, 1965.

Tackaberry, Andrew. *Famous Ghosts, Phantoms and Poltergeists for the Millions*. New York: Bell Publishing Co., 1947.

FURTHER READING AND WEBSITES

Ghosts of the White House
www.whitehouse.gov/ghosts
This is the place to find out all about the spirited inhabitants that have graced the U.S. president's official residence in Washington, D.C.

Gordon, Lawrence. *User Friendly*. Port St. Joe, FL: Karmichael Press, 1999. Fifteen-year-old Eddie Fields gets a new computer for his birthday. When mysterious messages start popping up on the monitor, Eddie realizes that a ghost is using the computer to communicate with him. As Eddie works to free the ghost from its restless afterlife, he learns the rules of the spirit world. Gordon follows this book with a sequel, *Haunted High*, in which Eddie teams up with paranormal researchers.

Herbst, Judith. *Beyond the Grave*. Minneapolis: Lerner Publications Company, 2005. In this book from The Unexplained series, Herbst describes stories and possible explanations for paranormal phenomena, including ghosts.

McNish, Cliff. *Breathe: A Ghost Story*. Minneapolis: Carolrhoda Books, 2006. After the sudden death of his father, Jack and his mother, Sarah, move in to an old farmhouse. Jack soon discovers that they are not alone. He—and only he—can see the ghosts of four children and the Ghost Mother who controls them. Jack must learn the secrets that keep these souls trapped in the house, before the Ghost Mother tries to take control of him and Sarah.

Mysterious Britain

http://www.mysteriousbritain.co.uk/hauntings/hauntingstemplate.html Merrie olde England doesn't look quite so cheerful on this site. "Ghosts and Hauntings in Britain" explores many of the supernatural tales that have been reported in the castles, homes, abbeys, and pubs of England, Scotland, and Wales.

Ruby, Laura. *Lily's Ghosts*. New York: Harper Collins, 2003. Lily and her mother move to Cape May, New Jersey, to live in the old Victorian mansion once owned by Lily's great-uncle Wes. Lily enjoys her new seaside town and makes a new friend. But her new house is another story. Lily isn't there long when she realizes that the house is full of ghosts. Understanding what the ghosts want from her draws Lily into a fifty-year family mystery.

Yee, Paul. *The Bone Collector's Son*. Tarrytown, NY: Marshall Cavendish, 2004. At the turn of the twentieth century, Bing lives with his immigrant father in the Chinatown section of Vancouver, a city in western Canada. He hates helping with his father's scary and disgusting job—collecting the bones of dead immigrants and shipping them back to China for proper burial. So Bing is thrilled when he is hired as a live-in servant for the wealthy Bentley family. But he discovers that his new job won't get him away from the dead. The Bentley home is haunted, and Bing must turn to his friends back in Chinatown to learn how to deal with the unhappy spirits.

MOVIES AND TV

Beetlejuice. Burbank, CA: Warner Home Video, 1988. This offbeat film tells a ghost story from the point of view of the ghosts. A gentle and kindhearted pair of spirits run into trouble when an obnoxious living family moves in to their home.

Disney's The Haunted Mansion. Burbank, CA: Buena Vista Home Entertainment, 2003. Workaholic real estate agent Jim Evers (Eddie Murphy) drags his wife and kids to see a creepy old mansion, Gracey Manor. When a big storm blows up, the family is forced to stay the night and is drawn into the mansion's mysteries.

Ghostbusters. Culver City, CA: Columbia TriStar Home Video, 1999. New York City seems to be attracting some powerful spirits and is in danger of becoming a paranormal disaster area. A team of ghostbusters steps in to try to save the city.

Ghost Hunters. This ongoing SciFi Channel show follows the adventures of a team of real-life paranormal investigators. The Atlantic Paranormal Society (TAPS) investigates reports of hauntings across the United States.

The Others. Burbank, CA: Dimension Films, 2002. A young mother and her children relocate to an isolated house during World War II. Once settled, the woman sees signs that the house is haunted and comes to believe that the ghosts want to harm her children.

INDEX

About the Author

Stephen Krensky is the author of many fiction and nonfiction books for children, including the On My Own Folklore series and *Bigfoot*, *The Bogeyman*, *Creatures from the Deep*, *Dragons*, *Frankenstein*, *The Mummy*, *Vampires*, *Watchers in the Woods*, *Werewolves*, and *Zombies*. When he isn't hunched over his computer, he makes school visits and teaches writing workshops. In his free time, he enjoys playing tennis and softball and reading books by other people. Krensky lives in Massachusetts with his wife, Joan, and their family.

Photo Acknowledgments

The images in this book are used with permission of: © Ann Ronan Picture Library/HIP/The Image Works, pp. 2–3; © D.C. Lowe/SuperStock, p. 11; © Time Life Pictures/Getty Images, p. 12; © Ramon Cavallo/AFP/Getty Images, p. 16; The Art Archive/John Meek, p. 18; © Fortean Picture Library, pp. 20, 22, 30; Mr. Harman, 2006, p. 25; © NMPFT/SSPL/The Image Works, p. 29; © Mary Evans Picture Library/The Image Works, p. 32; © Keystone Features/Hulton Archive/Getty Images, p. 33; © Pictorial Press Ltd/Alamy, p. 36; © Photofest, p. 38; POLTERGEIST © Turner Entertainment Co. A Warner Bros. Entertainment, Company. All Rights Reserved. Image provided by Photofest, p. 39; Courtesy of Universal Studios Licensing, LLLP. Image provided by Universal/Gordon/The Kobal Collection, p. 40; Courtesy of Universal Studios Licensing, LLLP. Image provided by Amblin/The Kobal Collection, p. 41; © CBS/Monty Brinton/Landov, p. 43. Illustrations © Bill Hauser/Independent Picture Service, pp. 1, 6–7, 9, 13, 17, 26, 34–35. All page background illustrations © Bill Hauser/Independent Picture Service.

Front cover: © Bill Hauser/Independent Picture Service.